SCHOLASTIC discover more™ stickers!

Penguins

LET'S STICK TOGETHER!

Use LOTS of stickers of penguin chicks to make a big group, called a crèche.

So cool, they're Antarctic

They're fat. They waddle when they walk. They have stumpy wings. But good news! Penguins look funny, but their bodies are perfect for where they live.

Arctic

Antarctica

Penguins live in the southern half of the world. The biggest ones live in Antarctica—nowhere near Santa or polar bears.

It's f-f-freezing in Antarctica! It is often -75ºF in the middle of the continent. You could freeze to death there even in SUMMER.

WHAT DO YOU CALL A PENGUIN IN THE ARCTIC?

Emperor penguins are the biggest penguins. Adults are about 50 inches tall. Is that bigger or smaller than you?

LOST. REALLY, REALLY LOST.

Penguins are tough birds! Their bodies help them stay warm.

blubber under the skin

Draw 300 dots here.

Penguin the size of this box.

That's how many feathers

there are on a patch of

tightly packed feathers

2

Meet the family

Match your stickers to the pictures!

fairy · Galápagos · chinstrap · Fiordland · erect-crested · rockhopper

Snares · Humboldt · African · Magellanic · royal

king · emperor · Adélie · gentoo · macaroni · yellow-eyed

THIS WAY ➡

Make a splash!

 webbed feet push away more water than toes do

 shaped just right to glide through water: fat in the middle, pointy at the ends

Penguins can't fly. ☹

But they can swim. ☺

Up to 25 miles per hour! 😃

Their sturdy wings are like flippers. 😄

In your face, robins! 😄 😄 😄

from below, a white tummy looks like light shining through the water

these birds can't fly, either

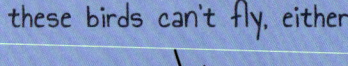

ostrich

cassowary

kiwi

kakapo

from above, a black back blends in with the dark ocean depths

WHERE DO PENGUINS GO SWIMMING?

AT THE SOUTH POOL.

Orcas and seals think penguins are pretty tasty. But before they can eat them . . . they have to find them! Penguins' feathers hide them from both above and below.

4

I CAN FLY!

COOOOOL FACT

PENGUINS SPEND 75% OF THEIR LIVES IN WATER.

TOP 10 swimming facts

Penguins' hearts slow down when they dive.

Penguins can dive down 1,800 feet.

Penguins can hold their breath underwater for 18 minutes.

Penguins swim faster by leaping in and out of the water. This is called porpoising.

Penguins can see well underwater.

Penguins hunch their heads into their shoulders when they swim.

Penguins take naps on the ocean's surface.

Penguins will swim up to 185 miles round-trip in search of a good meal.

Penguins can't swim backward.

Penguins use their feet and tails to steer.

Penguins spread special oil from their bodies over their feathers to waterproof them.

PORPOISING

Winter break!

Penguins don't need sleds on snow days. Waddling is slow . . . so when penguins have a need for speed, they flop down and slide across the ice and snow.

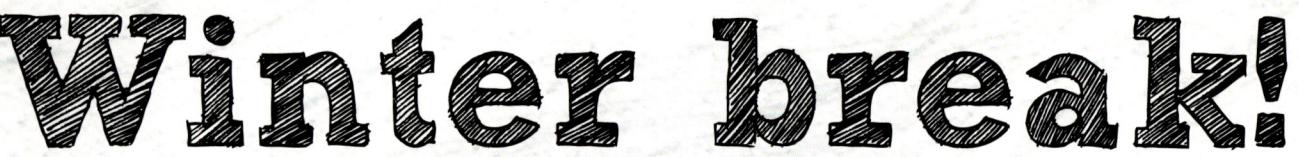

WHEEEEE!

Make a penguin race!

Add stickers of penguins tobogganing to make an icy race.

Watch out for rocks—OUCH!

Penguins on the go

FINISH

Penguins sway from side to side as they waddle on their short legs and big feet.

WHAT'S BLACK AND WHITE AND BLACK AND WHITE?

Who won? You decide! Put your three fastest penguins on the ice cubes.

A rockhopper can jump twice as high as its height. Beat that, humans!

A PENGUIN ROLLING DOWN A SNOWBANK!

1st 2nd 3rd

You're going to eat THAT?

Krill are tiny shrimp that taste delicious . . . which is kind of bad news for them.

Do you like sushi? Yes or no? Penguins like nothing better. They hurtle for miles across the ocean to grab fish, squid, and krill.

DRINKS
* seawater
* melted snow

APPETIZER
krill

MAIN COURSE

octopus

anchovies

squid

sardines

cuttlefish

SNACK
more krill

NO THANKS

penguins never eat vegetables

8

swimming penguin 1

swimming penguin 5

STICKERS
FOR
PAGES 4-5

Top 10

swimming penguin 2

swimming penguin 3

swimming penguin 4

swimming penguin, page 5

porpoising penguin

STICKERS
FOR
PAGES 6-7

STICKERS FOR PAGES 8–9

anchovies

sardines

squid

krill

cuttlefish

sardines

sardines

salt

pebbles

STICKERS FOR PAGES 10–11

gull

petrel

Polar bear

yellow mongoose

mole snake

leopard

dingo

safe penguins

STICKERS FOR PAGES 12-13

leaping penguin

leaping penguin

waddling penguins

tobogganing penguin

tobogganing penguin

egg

STICKERS FOR PAGES 14-15

Seriously GROSS

Brace yourself. A penguin's table manners are even worse than your kid brother's.

Penguins don't pee. That would waste water!

Penguin babies eat food that Mom or Dad has spit up.

penguin poop is white and thick like a paste

Penguins eat their food alive (and usually wriggling). Spines inside their mouths keep anything from escaping.

pebbles

salt

sardines

Penguins don't have teeth. They swallow small stones to grind up their food.

▶▶ **COOOOOL FACT**

PENGUINS DRINK SALTY SEAWATER, THEN

DRIP THE SALT OUT OF LITTLE HOLES IN THEIR BEAKS.

Look out!

Seabirds will snatch up an egg or a chick, but most penguin predators live in the water. Seals and orcas watch a penguin flipping through the water and see just one thing: dinner!

Leopard seals hide under ice shelves, waiting for penguins to dive in. Then these big, fast hunters go in for the kill.

Sneaky gulls may work in pairs. One threatens a penguin parent while the other steals its egg.

gull

WHAT DID THE OCEAN SAY TO THE SHORE?

AFTER YOU ...

NO, AFTER YOU ...

NO, AFTER YOU ...

Fill the ocean with stickers of penguin predators and scared penguins.

NOTHING. IT JUST WAVED.

petrel

Giant petrels are also called stinkers—for good reason. They can peck penguins to death with their sharp, stabbing bills.

There's a **predator** near ...

All kinds of animals go after the eggs and chicks of the penguins that live north of Antarctica.

yellow mongoose   mole snake   leopard   dingo

safe penguins

Polar bears don't eat penguins. They don't live anywhere near penguins!

MYTH BUSTER!

A penguin can outrun a leopard seal on land.

orca

An orca (also called a killer whale) weighs up to 12,000 pounds. It has a mouthful of big, sharp teeth. Orcas often work in pods, or groups, to hunt down penguins.

The loooooong cold

cold →

When winter is coming, emperor penguins waddle 70 miles to their breeding grounds. Then the dads hold the eggs on their feet . . . for two months, standing up, in temperatures as low as -75°F.

Antarctica in Winter

← -75°F (CRAZY COLD!)

ARE WE THERE YET?

ocean 50 miles

leaping

The penguins travel single file, nonstop, day and night.

waddling

tobogganing

TRUE ♥ LOVE

At the breeding grounds, Mom lays one egg. She carefully passes it from her feet to Dad's feet. Then she turns and heads back to the water.

ACTUAL SIZE →

Keep your hands at your sides and pass a ball from the tops of your feet to the tops of your friend's feet. Don't let it touch the ground or it will freeze!

12

march

breeding 20
ground miles

Emperor dads stand with their eggs for two months. They cover the eggs with warm skin.

HOW DO SNOWMEN TRAVEL AROUND?

BY ICICLE!

reaching the breeding ground

The dads huddle together for warmth. Use your stickers to make a big, big huddle!

All together

See me grow

Great. Of all the places to be born—Antarctica in winter. At least Dad keeps me warm.

Mom's back with food. She's spitting up chewed fish? Oh! It's delicious!

Mom and Dad went to get me more fish. I'm huddling with my friends to keep warm.

DON'T LOOK AT ME! I'm losing my fluff! But at least I'm getting my sea feathers. Soon I can go swimming!

A fluffy newborn emperor chick snuggles against Dad. Then Mom comes back with food—to spit into its mouth!

Make an emperor penguin colony with LOTS of dads, moms, and chicks.

Moms and dads look after their chicks until the chicks get sea feathers and can go fishing by themselves. There can be 3,000 families living together in a colony!

SAY "FISH"!

ISBN 978-0-545-61231-9

10 9 8 7 6 5 4 3 2 1   14 15 16 17 18

Printed in Malaysia   106
First edition, January 2014

Image credits

Book pages
1 (background): malerapaso/iStockphoto; 1 (chicks): Vladsilver/Dreamstime; 1 (sign br, used throughout): inxti/Shutterstock; 2-3 (blue icicles): Merzavka/iStockphoto; 2-3 (background): DLILLC/Media Bakery; 2 (Santa hat): apdesign/Shutterstock; 2 (cartoon penguin bl): Scholastic Inc.; 2-3 (all other cartoon penguins): Randy Glasbergen/glasbergen.com; 2br: Starper/Dreamstime; 3 (tracks tr): tereez/Shutterstock; 3 (blue sign): mythja/Shutterstock; 3 (sign br): Osipovfoto/Shutterstock; 4-5 (background): Hemera/Thinkstock; 4-5 (photo corners, used throughout): hanibaram/iStockphoto; 4 (penguin tl): Isselee/Dreamstime; 4 (ostrich): Mlenny/iStockphoto; 4 (cassowary): Melonesaj/Dreamstime; 4 (kiwi): Tui De Roy/Corbis Images; 4 (kakapo): ANT Photo Library/Science Source; 4 (penguin bl): Julien Tromeur/Shutterstock; 5 (cartoon penguins): Randy Glasbergen/glasbergen.com; 5 (plane): Kamira/Shutterstock; 5 (photo tr): Ivantihelka/Dreamstime; 5 (oil drip): dp3010/iStockphoto; 5 (paper background, used throughout): hudiemm/iStockphoto; 5 (photo br): Joshanon1/Dreamstime; 5 (penguin br): Julien Tromeur/Shutterstock; 6-7 (background): Stab/Dreamstime; 6-7 (snowy rocks): PinkBadger/iStockphoto, Fallsview/Dreamstime; 6-7 (piled snow): ThingsofNature/Dreamstime; 6-7 (tobogganing penguins t): Silver/Fotolia; 6-7 (flags): iStockphoto/Thinkstock; 6 (cartoon penguin): Randy Glasbergen/glasbergen.com; 6 (penguins bl): Coldimages/iStockphoto; 6 (tobogganing penguins b): Gentoomultimedia/Dreamstime; 7 (penguins under sign): Coldimages/iStockphoto; 7 (photo tc): Bernard Breton/Dreamstime; 7 (photo cm): Fuse/Thinkstock; 7 (penguin cr): RichLindie/iStockphoto; 7 (large rock r): Samot/Shutterstock; 7 (ice cubes): sbayram/iStockphoto; 7 (ribbons): Graffizone/iStockphoto; 7 (penguin br): Janelle Lugge/Shutterstock; 8-9 (dripping paint t): legalALIEN/iStockphoto; 8-9 (background): SilverV/iStockphoto; 8-9 (paint blobs): Eratel/iStockphoto; 8 (glass): lenazap/iStockphoto; 8 (photo tr): Tom McHugh/Science Source; 8 (plate): t_kimura/iStockphoto; 8 (octopus): Stasis Photo/Shutterstock; 8 (fork): eli_asenova/iStockphoto; 8 (penguins tl): Coldimages/iStockphoto; 9 (penguin tr): Julien Tromeur/Shutterstock; 9 (toilet paper): dlerick/iStockphoto; 9 (toilet): LokFung/iStockphoto; 9 (photo t): William Ervin/iStockphoto; 9 (photo b): gary yim/Shutterstock; 9 (large penguin with fish): Micha Klootwijk/Shutterstock; 10-11 (background t): Triff/Shutterstock; 10-11 (background b): Mlenny/iStockphoto; 10 (photo l): Robert W. Hernandez/Science Source; 10 (seal): ekvals/iStockphoto; 10 (icebergs): GibasDigiPhoto/iStockphoto; 10-11 (cartoon

penguins): Randy Glasbergen/glasbergen.com; 11 (seal): mike_matas/iStockphoto; 11br: datmore/iStockphoto; 12-13 (background t): dmax-foto/iStockphoto; 12-13 (blue icicles): Merzavka/iStockphoto; 12 (thermometer): lineartestpilot/Shutterstock; 12 (cartoon penguin): Randy Glasbergen/glasbergen.com; 12 (penguin holding sign): Julien Tromeur/Shutterstock; 12 (photo l): Gentoomultimedia/Dreamstime; 12 (walking penguin r): Freezingpictures/Dreamstime; 12 (hearts): ulimi/iStockphoto; 12 (penguins bl): Staphy/Dreamstime; 12 (egg): Keren Su/Lonely Planet Images/Getty Images; 12-13 (signpost c): ZargonDesign/iStockphoto; 13tr: Doug Allan/The Image Bank/Getty Images; 13 (walking penguins l): J.-L. Klein & M.-L. Hubert/Science Source; 13 (photo r): Arco Images GmbH/Alamy; 13bc: Kim Westerskov/Getty Images; 14-15 (background): Evgeny Kovalev spb/Shutterstock; 14-15 (snowy bottom, adult penguin b): iStockphoto/Thinkstock; 14 (photo t): KeithSzafranski/iStockphoto; 14 (photo ct): Greg Dimijian/Science Source; 14 (photo cb): blickwinkel/Poelking/Alamy; 14 (photo b): Bryan and Cherry Alexander/Science Source; 15 (penguins t): Staphy/Dreamstime; 15 (chicks br): Vladsilver/Dreamstime; 16 (balloon): Flynt/Dreamstime; 16 (cartoon penguin): Randy Glasbergen/glasbergen.com; 16 (photo t): Mint_Images/iStockphoto; all others: Scholastic Inc.

Sticker pages
Sticker page 1: (penguins holding signs, used throughout) Sebastian Kaulitzki/Shutterstock; (chicks) Silver/Fotolia, Mint_Images/iStockphoto, iStockphoto/Thinkstock, Coldimages/iStockphoto; (adult penguin) Coldimages/iStockphoto; (balloon) Flynt/Dreamstime; (fairy) Inaras/Dreamstime; (Galápagos) jmmf/iStockphoto; (Adélie) flammulated/iStockphoto; (Fiordland) Cmfotoworks/Dreamstime; (erect-crested) Bertys30/Dreamstime; (yellow-eyed) StephanHoerold/iStockphoto; (emperor) Staphy/Dreamstime; (Humboldt) Eric Isselee/Shutterstock; (African) Isselee/Dreamstime; (gentoo) leksele/iStockphoto; (Snares) Janelle Lugge/Shutterstock; (penguin, page 2) Coldimages/iStockphoto; (king) Photomaru/Dreamstime; (royal) Art Wolfe/Science Source; (chinstrap) MOF/iStockphoto; (Magellanic) Yevgenia Gorbulsky/Shutterstock; (macaroni) John Shaw/Science Source; (rockhopper) RichLindie/iStockphoto. Sticker page 2: (penguins in glasses) Julien Tromeur/Shutterstock; (porpoising penguin) Joshanon1/Dreamstime; (swimming penguin, page 5) Ivantihelka/Dreamstime; (all other swimming penguins) Isselee/Dreamstime; (penguin with snorkel) Julien Tromeur/Shutterstock; (tobogganing penguins) Gentoomultimedia/Dreamstime, Silver/Fotolia, Fuse/Thinkstock; (adults with chicks) KeithSzafranski/

iStockphoto; (chick) Mint_Images/iStockphoto; (small penguins) Inaras/Dreamstime, Yevgenia Gorbulsky/Shutterstock, jmmf/iStockphoto, Isselee/Dreamstime, flammulated/iStockphoto, Janelle Lugge/Shutterstock, RichLindie/iStockphoto, MOF/iStockphoto, Bertys30/Dreamstime; (large penguins) Photomaru/Dreamstime, Coldimages/iStockphoto, leksele/iStockphoto; (petrel) serengeti130/iStockphoto. Sticker page 3: (squid) Wksp/Dreamstime; (krill) Minden Pictures/SuperStock; (anchovies) PicturePartners/iStockphoto; (sardines) Eyeblink/Dreamstime; (salt) malerapaso/iStockphoto; (fish skeletons) lineartestpilot/Shutterstock; (cuttlefish) Wksp/Dreamstime; (pebbles) Juanmonino/iStockphoto; (broccoli) eli_asenova/iStockphoto; (paint) Eratel/iStockphoto; (gull) Roy Toft/National Geographic/Getty Images; (swimming Humboldts) Isselee/Dreamstime; (petrels) serengeti130/iStockphoto; (mongoose) Mendelewski/iStockphoto; (snake) Fouroaks/Dreamstime; (leopard) Peter ten Broecke/iStockphoto; (dingo) kaniwi/iStockphoto; (polar bear) JackF/iStockphoto; (seal head) BMJ/Shutterstock; (swimming emperors) VMJones/iStockphoto; (seal) Llandrea/Dreamstime; (walking emperors) Coldimages/iStockphoto; (orca) jandaly/iStockphoto. Sticker page 4: (leaping penguins, tobogganing penguins) Gentoomultimedia/Dreamstime; (huddled penguins) Kim Westerskov/Getty Images; (egg) Keren Su/Lonely Planet Images/Getty Images; (waddling penguins) J.-L. Klein & M.-L. Hubert/Science Source, Freezingpictures/Dreamstime; (petrel) serengeti130/iStockphoto; (adults) Coldimages/iStockphoto; (chicks) iStockphoto/Thinkstock, Mint_Images/iStockphoto, Silver/Fotolia; (adults with chicks) KeithSzafranski/iStockphoto; (swimming penguins) VMJones/iStockphoto. All others: Scholastic Inc.

Cover
Front cover: (main image) Frans Lanting/Corbis Images; (background) Mike Hill/Oxford Scientific/Getty Images; (bl) Duncan Noakes/Dreamstime; (bcl) Gentoomultimedia/Dreamstime; (bcr) RichLindie/iStockphoto; (br) KeithSzafranski/iStockphoto. Back cover: (background t) pkline/iStockphoto; (background b) Mlenny/iStockphoto; (snowflakes) Irochka_T/iStockphoto; (penguins, top row, l to r) MOF/iStockphoto, AlesVeluscek/iStockphoto, flammulated/iStockphoto, Brandon Smith/Dreamstime, Yevgenia Gorbulsky/Shutterstock, Eric Isselee/Shutterstock; (cl) VMJones/iStockphoto; (cr, chick br) KeithSzafranski/iStockphoto; (cartoon penguin br) Scholastic Inc.